HEAVENLY MEANINGS: THE PARABLES OF JESUS

COMPILED BY HAYES PRESS

Published by:

HAYES PRESS Publisher, Resources & Media,

The Barn, Flaxlands

Royal Wootton Bassett

Swindon, SN4 8DY

United Kingdom

If you enjoy reading this book and/or others in the series, we would really appreciate it if you could just take a couple of minutes to leave a brief review where you purchased this book.

CHAPTER ONE: INTRODUCTION

MUCH TEACHING IN THE Scriptures, both in the Old Testament and in the New, is presented to us in figurative and symbolic forms. Eastern languages lend themselves readily to figurative forms of speech, so we find much use being made of types, similitudes, proverbs, allegories and parables.

The use of appropriate illustrations is a valuable aid in the teaching process. Good illustrations act like windows, letting in light to illuminate the mind. Apt illustrations remain imprinted in the memory long after they have been heard, and they are readily recalled. The use of parable, therefore, constitutes a valuable and enduring form of instruction. The effectiveness of the use of a parable to impart a message to the hearer is well illustrated by the parable Nathan told to David to convict him of his great sin (2 Samuel 12:1-15). David was quick to pronounce judgement on the man depicted in the parable, and when it was brought home to him that he was the man portrayed in the narrative he could not but confess, "I have sinned against the LORD".

Solomon, in his day, made extensive use of proverbs and parables in his teaching, and men and women came from far and near to hear the wisdom that God had put in his heart. The books of Proverbs and Ecclesiastes give us some of that distilled wisdom. He drew his illustrations from the whole field of nature and delighted his audiences with the choice words that he used in his teaching (1 Kings 4:32,33; Ecclesiastes 12:9,10), but when the Lord Jesus was here on earth a greater than Solomon was here among men (Matthew 12:42).

The Lord Jesus was a matchless teacher. The multitudes were astonished at His teaching "for He taught them as One having authority" (Matthew

Table of Contents

7:28,29). His fellow countrymen asked. "Whence hath this Man this wisdom?" (Matthew 13:54), and men sent to arrest Him were disarmed by His teaching and exclaimed, "Never man so spake" (John 7:46). However, they failed to appreciate that He was more than Man and that in Him were all the treasures of wisdom and knowledge hidden (Colossians 2:3).

Early in His ministry the Lord gave plain direct teaching, but as it became evident that His teaching was unacceptable to the leaders of the nation, He began to teach by parables, and in so doing He fulfilled the prophecies of Isaiah 6:10 and Psalm 78:2 (see John 12:39-41; Matthew 13:34,35). His disciples asked Him why He was speaking in parables. His answer revealed that He was doing so to hide from His hearers the knowledge of truths that they were not in a condition to receive, but they were also spoken to instruct those whose attitude of heart would enable them to profit from His teaching (Matthew 13:10-16).

The word "parable" (Greek: 'parabole') signifies a placing of one thing beside another with a view to comparison (W.E. Vine). It is generally used of a short descriptive narrative drawn from nature or human circumstances for the purpose of illustrating and setting forth spiritual truth. In the synoptic gospels the word is also used in relation to a short saying or proverb (e.g. Matthew 15:11,15; Luke 4:23;6:39). The parable differs from the fable in that it never transgresses the natural order of things by attributing reason and speech to trees, birds and beasts. It may also be distinguished from the allegory, which is a more elaborate form of illustration in which a comparison is to be found in all or most of the details given.

The Lord Jesus never used fables in His teaching; the use of fables would not have been in keeping with the lofty and authoritative standard of His teaching. The many parables that He told dealt with matters of fact, with common everyday events or with the operation of the laws of nature, and who better than He who is the Creator to show the harmony that there is between the laws of nature and spiritual truths.

The Lord narrated His parables in such a way that His audiences were enthralled; they appreciated the beauty of the stories and the moral teaching that lay on the surface, but the deeper spiritual truths underlying them were hidden from them. What we have in our Bibles are sometimes synopses of the accounts that were given to the multitudes, yet the beauty of the narratives comes through even in our English translations. The interpretations of the parables were given in private sessions to the disciples (Mark 4:10,34; Matthew 13:36), but even so there was much that they did not understand. The Lord gave them such instruction as they were able to bear while He was with them (John 16:12). After His resurrection in those private teaching sessions He had with them He was able to tell them more (Luke 24:44-49; Acts 1:3), but for a fuller enlightenment they had to await the coming of the Holy Spirit (John 16:13-16). The Holy Spirit subsequently brought to their remembrance the Lord's words and enlightened their minds (John 14:26). The Lord's teaching given through the medium of His parables would be among the things of which the Holy Spirit would give them a fuller understanding; we should expect, therefore, to find an amplification of the truths underlying the parables in the teaching given in the epistles and this will be explored in our study of the parables.

The parables the Lord told, of which more than thirty are recorded, are to be found in the synoptic gospels, Matthew, Mark and Luke. In John's Gospel there is no mention of a parable although much figurative language is used in the form of metaphor and allegory, and the Lord represents Himself for example, as the Good Shepherd, the Door, the True Vine, and the Light of the World.

A few of the Lord's parables were addressed to individuals, some were addressed to His disciples, either in private or in the hearing of the multitudes, but most were delivered in the course of His general teaching to the multitudes, and in some instances we are given the specific reason for the telling of a particular parable. There are many precious lessons to be learned from a study of the parables; some are easier to interpret than others, but the great need in every case is the illumination that the Holy Spirit gives to the earnest seeker after truth.

The subject matter covered in the parables is wide-ranging and so are the divine principles and spiritual truths illustrated by them. It is our purpose to examine these in a series of chapters contributed by a variety of writers. We shall find in the parables truths relating to the involvement of the Trinity in the redemption of man; principles relating to prayer, forgiveness, faithfulness, service and its rewards, and warnings against pride, covetousness and materialism. The accountability of those in positions of responsibility and privilege and the outworking of age long divine purposes are also set out in them. These and 'many other things besides will be' examined in our study of the parables. The need to put into practice what we learn and not be only hearers of the Word, but also doers, is stressed in the story that the Lord told of the builders on rock and on earth (Luke 6:46-49). We should be ever mindful of the consequences of failing to so build.

CHAPTER TWO: A THREE-FOLD PARABLE

THE LORD JESUS, GREATEST Teacher of all time with perfect understanding of earthly things as well as heavenly (John 3:12), conveys in simple terms and easily understandable literary style, profound spiritual truths in the trilogy of Luke 15. This Gospel is one of gladness. Joy and happiness are major themes throughout its historical account. The parable might be fittingly titled "Lost and Found". The Lord's audience was a mixed one. Those who were despised and sinful, conscious of the need for repentance and having the desire for forgiveness, came to Him: self-righteous rulers and authorities criticized Him. The latter forfeited the benefit of the Lord's reception and welcome.

The three stories are one parable (v.3). They represent the total picture of humanity's fallen condition and lost state - the sheep lost itself, the silver lost by its possessor, the son lost to his father. Common features appear: three persons suffering loss; the first losing an animal, the second an object, the last someone precious. Searching and seeking, the joy of finding and resultant celebrations are shared by all three. The love of the Father, Son and Spirit is illustrated in the separate incidents. The sheep was in need of help from its provider, the silver possessed value to its owner and the son required love and forgiveness from his parent. In the first incident we find shelter and security where there was sorrow and fear; the second moves from silence and worry to shouting and triumph; the third from famine to feasting.

The Lost Sheep

One missing out of a hundred might appear hardly worth the effort of long and difficult searching, but not one single animal of creation escapes the attention and watchfulness of a faithful Creator. He ensures the food supply of the birds of heaven (Matthew 6:26; Job 38:41). Their death He individually notes (Matthew 10:29). People are of infinitely more value. Each sheep was of value to the shepherd. One lost meant the shepherd's going out, having first provided adequate care for those remaining. The Son of Man came to seek and save the lost. His commission to His apostles was to go to the lost sheep of the house of Israel (Matthew 10:16). The nation as a whole and every single individual in it had gone astray, wilfully turning aside (Isaiah 53:6). Only the long-promised and long-awaited Messiah had the desire and the ability to do something about it. Finding the lost involved for Him suffering and anguish, crossing some of the pitiless terrain of this world, and collecting wounds, bruises and scars in the painstaking labour of love to locate the lost. These involved Calvary experiences, suffering for those whose loss was self-inflicted. The shepherd knew the appearance, habits and personality of the missing sheep. He went after it no matter the cost until he found it. The cost of redemption, the price of salvation, the sacrifice for sin are all here. This story also illustrates the sad plight of the self-righteous Pharisees and scribes. The Lord could not call the righteous for there was none. They were convicted as they listened.

How long did the shepherd spend searching and to what extent did he suffer? These details are not recorded. We shall never be able to evaluate completely the cost and suffering of our Saviour, Shepherd and Lord. To Him each individual sheep was precious, valuable, and the object of His saving love. Those who remain ignorant of their lost state can never be saved. Everyone is in need of repentance. Joy is not only in the heart of the Finder but that of His friends. The elation of verses 6 and 7 recalls the lovely phrases of Isaiah 53:10 and 11. The shepherd's gladness, the sheep's restoration, the joy of others clearly depict the Redeemer's joy, the sinner's forgiveness and the angels' delight when one sinner is "found".

The Lost Silver

In the second story the loss sustained is substantially more (ten per cent as opposed to one per cent). Silver is a valuable commodity in the world. Its monetary appeal is often referred to in Scripture, in many instances contrasting with the greater worth of God's work and Word (Psalm 119:72; Acts 3:6). There is no let-up of activity until the missing piece is found: the lamp lit, the house cleaned, a diligent search undertaken of the whole area. These clearly portray the sovereign work of God and the movement of the Spirit of God. The work of "recovery" where darkness and blindness is present is attributed to this divine Person in Luke 4:18. The power of the Spirit was so evident in the Lord Jesus "... I by the Finger of God cast out ..." (Luke 11:20). Blasphemously, some attributed the Lord's acts to the activity of Satan and were thus guilty of an unforgivable sin (Luke 12:10). The Spirit uses the Word of God - the lamp (Psalm 119:105) which exposes sin, analyses our need and illuminates the way of salvation. His constant activity is focused on the value of the sinner-soul, exposing his unrighteousness, illuminating and declaring the Saviour whose person He glorifies (see John chapters 14 and 16). He is a Searcher and Revealer (1 Corinthians 2:10,12). His sovereign and diligent exercises in salvation are beautifully and graphically illustrated in this woman's pursuit of a valuable but' lost item. His motivation is pure divine love. That love is shed abroad (or "Poured Out within" NASB) in the believer's heart (Romans 5:5). Joy abounds in heaven as well as on earth over each sinner who repents.

The Lost Son

Who would deny the glorious truth of the Father's love in this story? It is a story of love that covers those lost through sin. Sin is selfish ("give me"); alienates from God ("a far country"); destroys ("wasted his substance"); robs ("began to be in want"); devastates and ultimately kills ("I perish"). What a contrast this story is to the Son of the Father's love

(Colossians 1:13), who never for one moment caused grief to His Father. The distinction here from the precious stories is the showing of the steps to repentance before the exercise of faith. Only when he was left with nothing (v.14) did he find himself in a world with nothing to offer that will last; a place of famine, friendships evaporating at the same rate as his money. Being joined to a stranger was hard enough, but to feed unclean animals was worse and strictly forbidden to this formerly wealthy Jewish son (Leviticus 11:7,8). His shame, need and sense of being lost were great, "no man gave unto him".

The realization of perishing awakened him to thoughts of the father and the need for home. "I will go to my father" (v.18). Convicted of his sin firstly against God, he cried, like David (Psalm 51:4). He needed mercy, he was worthy of death as a riotous liver (Deuteronomy 21:20). The father had been offended, but this did not affect his love. He was waiting, looking, searching. His eyes had never left that road of repentance and return. The father saw him, his heart filled up, his eyes watered, he ran and embraced him. Ephesians 2:4-9 touches a chord in every redeemed heart. Excuses were futile, repentance was necessary, confession made; "I have sinned". Nothing less, nothing more required. Between themselves the issue is resolved, then the son is brought back into the house (v.22). From rags of sin to riches of grace in a robe of righteousness (Isaiah 61:10). It was the best suit - God's work is never less than perfect. The ring symbolizes the pledge of the father's love, in salvation the unique gift of the indwelling Holy Spirit (Ephesians 1:13,14), pledge of future complete and final possession. The shoes take us to service in sonship responsibility. The fatted calf, the riches of the Father's provision in Christ - "in Him ye are made full" (Colossians 2:10). Great joy follows; it has no ending; so will our eternal glory be in Christ.

In this parable is revealed by the Son the love and joy of deity in a way no human mind or fleshly heart could expound. Only the Son, who is in the bosom of the Father, has the capacity to unfold the intimate emotions of the three Persons of the Godhead.

> Glory to the Holy Three,
>
> Father, Son and Spirit be;
>
> Him who gave, and Him who died,
>
> Him who with us doth abide.

CHAPTER THREE: THE GOOD SAMARITAN

———

UNDER THE OLD COVENANT in Israel, eternal life was secured, not by rigidly adhering to a set of rules called the Law, but by a relationship with God based on faith. Obedience to God in keeping the Law was evidence of the relationship that existed. Thus, when the lawyer responded to his own question in Luke 10 about how to inherit eternal life, his answer was an appropriate summary of the Law.

The Lord Himself said the same thing when in Mark 12 He was asked "What commandment is the foremost of all?" His answer was that which the lawyer gave: "You shall love the Lord your God ... and your neighbor as yourself". To the lawyer in Matthew 22:40 He said: "On these two commandments depend the whole Law and the Prophets". Without a relationship with God based on faith in whatever generation, eternal life is not possible. The Law is not a formula for eternal life. It points man to the One who gives eternal life, God Himself. Rigid adherence to a legal system, as taught by the leaders in Israel, never purchased eternal life. The Lord abhorred merely formal observance of tradition and condemned Israel for it.

What is eternal life? The Lord Jesus defined it in John 17:3 where we read: "And this is eternal life, that they may know Thee, the only true God, and Jesus Christ whom Thou hast sent". It is not simply a measure of the length of life, but it is a new life with new qualities based on a personal relationship with the eternal God, and given by Him to those who come to Him by faith in His Word (Romans 6:23). Hebrews 11:6 makes it clear that in any generation "without faith it is impossible to please Him". The scribe in Mark 12:34 realized that a legal system was of no use without the intended relationship through faith and love. To him the Lord said, "You are not far from the kingdom of God". The system that was put in place was of continuous value, but each person had to be united to it by faith (Hebrews 4:2).

A relationship of love with God demands an application to men. The apostle John later wrote to fellow disciples of the Lord and said that if someone says "I love God", and hates his brother, he is a liar; for the one who does not love his brother whom he has seen, cannot love God whom he has not seen. And this commandment we have from Him, that the one who loves God should love his brother also" (1 John 4:20,21).

One cannot claim to love those whom God loves, other men and women. It is not only the Law that insists that people show love to one another, but the New Covenant has the same requirement for us. The lawyer, no doubt, believed he knew and loved God as he should. But he obviously did not understand what was involved. The teachers of the day restricted the meaning of neighbor to include very few. So he asked, "And who is my neighbor?" The lawyer could recite the words of the Law, but had little concept of its practical implications. He was about to learn how far short of God's standard he and his nation fell in their keeping of the Law. And he was about to see a beautiful picture of the mercy of God in Christ.

The identity of the man who fell among robbers is not given, perhaps since Christ was about to point out that one's nationality and religion had nothing to do with being a neighbor. As he travelled, he was beaten and left for dead. As a priest of the house of God, the first passerby certainly knew the Law and his responsibility to keep it. His condition before God should have complemented his position in the house of God (the same remains true today). Yet this spiritual leader passed by the one on whom he should have shown mercy. Though he knew the Law, his love for God was not what it should have been to compel him to come to the aid of the fallen man.

The Levite who passed by a short time later was also a man whose occupation brought him in touch with the holy things of God. His activities in the house of God, at the very heart of the place of service, should have been the mirror of his, affection and reverence for God. His lack of mercy for the one in need shows otherwise. He valued his position in the house of God, without guarding his condition: a danger in our day as well.

The Lord was not implying that every priest and Levite was without compassion. But he was showing that the legal system these men represented was not the means of salvation. The law was not wrong; the condition of the people was. In fact, as Paul later wrote, "The Law is holy, and the commandment is holy and righteous and good" (Romans 7:12). But the people were unable to keep the Law due to weakness of the flesh (Romans 8:3). Their self-righteousness kept them from true righteousness which a relationship with God would have given them.

The Samaritan was despised by the Jews, an outcast of their society. Yet, in the Lord's story, the Samaritan saw the beaten man, and without regard for his own safety, ensured appropriate care was given and proper provision was made. This was significant to the Jewish lawyer. His own people had passed by. Yet here was one whom he despised who stopped and fulfilled the true meaning of the Law without regard to race or status. To the question, "Which of these three do you think proved to be a neighbor to the man who fell into the robbers' hands?" he replied "The one who showed mercy toward him". And Jesus said to him, "Go and do the same". He would only be able to do so after humbling himself before God.

The one whom the lawyer rejected as a neighbor in his teaching was the very one whom the Lord showed to be a neighbor in His teaching. The lawyer had sought to justify himself with his scholarly questions. Yet he was brought face to face with his own shortcomings and those of his people in their keeping of the Law. Eternal life is not simply a scholarly matter. It is a matter of the heart that has been made aware of its sinful condition, and aware of the One who has taken a dealing with that sin.

Paul wrote, "Therefore the Law has become our tutor to lead us to Christ, that we may be justified by faith" (Galatians 3:24). Upon recognition of his own weakness to keep the Law, this man would have done well to enquire further about Christ. He might have asked, as did the man who came to Christ in Matthew 19, "What am I still lacking?" He was told to give up his earthly treasures "and come, follow Me". The man in Matthew felt he had kept the Law. This lawyer no doubt knew that he had not. Both needed Christ. The Law could not save.

On another level, this parable illustrates another Man who was despised and rejected by the Jews, the Lord Jesus Christ. He came to where we were, totally unable to save ourselves, and lifted us up from death to life. Religious formality is powerless to save in any generation. Yet He is One who displayed rich mercy in saving us and bringing us to a place of rest where care can be provided. He paid the price in order for that care to be provided and has promised to return with further reward. The Lord did that for us without regard for nationality, religion, or social status. He became our neighbor, needy as we were and unable to save ourselves.

This parable speaks further at another level: that is, the neighborly example of the Samaritan to those of us who have a relationship with God. Formal religious behavior that is based on the hollow traditions of men does not please God. Furthermore, even the habitual following of scriptural doctrines, without a love for the Lord and a desire to please Him, is not pleasing to Him. Such are illustrated by the example of the priest and the Levite. Their occupation in the house of God was commendable, but their spiritual condition was deplorable. Men will know that we are disciples of the Lord Jesus Christ if we show love for each other.

Paul writes to disciples of the Lord and says: "Now we who are strong ought to bear the weaknesses of those without strength and not just please ourselves. Let each of us please his neighbor for his good, to his edification. For even Christ did not please Himself" (Romans 15:1-3). To the Corinthians he writes: "Let no one seek his own good, but that of his neighbor" (1 Corinthians 10:24). Our neighbor is the one who needs our help. Ours is not to choose where and when we serve, but whom we serve. That will dictate the where and when. And we will be empowered by the Holy Spirit to be neighbors who show the mercy of God to those who are in need of it.

The parable of the Good Samaritan instructs us at three levels: firstly, that eternal life is the result of relationship, not rules, for "if righteousness comes through the Law, then Christ died needlessly" (Galatians 2:21); secondly, that Christ is the One who became our neighbor to lift us from death to life and bring us to a place of care and rest; and thirdly, that disciples of the Lord Jesus Christ should show that neighborly, Christ-like character as we "Bear one another's burdens, and thus fulfil the law of Christ" (Galatians 6:2).

CHAPTER FOUR: THE SOWER

THERE IS A SENSE IN which the sun is hidden by a piece of smoked glass and yet without such it is often not possible to look at the sun at all. So Christ taught and revealed by illustration. Some familiar thing of earth was placed alongside some mysterious thing of heaven that our understanding of the one might help us to understand the other. Christ never attempted to hide the truth from those who were ready to hear. His parables were an aid rather than a hindrance.

The Lord's disciples had received Jesus Christ as Saviour, Lord and King and by reason of that they were able to receive the mysteries of the kingdom. For the most part the Jews had rejected Christ as their Messiah and King and without the King they had no key to the mysteries of the kingdom. Because of this, in infinite pity and grace, He addressed them in parables. This was such a method of teaching as would constrain those who were undecided to see and hear. It was adopted in grace to meet the need of their nearsightedness.

The Outline

The seven parables of Matthew 13 relate generally to conditions obtaining between that moment in which He spoke and the consummation of the age. The first four were apparently spoken outside the house where He was staying, to the multitude of people who stood on the beach. The latter three, together with the interpretation of the parable of the tares, were spoken inside the house privately to His disciples.

The first of these parables, the parable of the sower, is not introduced, as are the others, by any reference to the kingdom, although that follows later in the, chapter. It is the story of the initial work of sowing.

Subsequently, and in a series of parables, the Lord proceeded to refer to the issues of that work. In each case the story itself was simple to interpret and the figurative terms He employed, such as the seed, were consistently used.

This is one of two parables which the Lord explained. The other is the parable of the tares of the field. It is obviously fundamental because He said that if men were unable to understand this one they could not understand the others (see Mark 4:13).

The Parable

The parable refers to the kingdom of heaven in Matthew and to the kingdom of God in both Mark and Luke. It is not our intention to deal at length with comparison and contrast in relation to these kingdoms. It is sufficient to say that the issue of the parable is evidently equally relevant whether we are considering the particular sphere of Christ's rule as Lord in the subject hearts of the kingdom of God or in the sphere of God's rule in the kingdom of heaven.

The work of the King was to scatter seed to produce results for the kingdom. The work of the enemy was to attempt to prevent results by injury to the seed because of the soil into which it fell. Such is the continuing conflict in which, it appears, failure predominates because "the whole world lieth in the evil one" (1 John 5:19). The picture is perfectly natural by eastern standards. In "The Land and the Book" by Dr. Thomson, the sower is said to have lived in a hamlet and did not sow adjacent to his house. He "went forth" into open country where there are paths, thorns, rocks and fertile places. There was, therefore, a trampling down by passers-by, and birds picked up the seed. The farmer worked with the mattock rather than the plough near to rocky places so that there was no depth there to the soil. Some of the most tangled of thorn bushes grew in such areas. So the sower sowed one kind of seed into different kinds of soil and the sequence of events thereafter depended on the nature of the soil.

The Teaching

The Lord makes no reference in His explanation to the sower himself. The main focus of the parable is on the reception by the soil of the seed that was sown. The soil is the heart of a person in his age and generation and the introduction of the seed, the Word of God, is that which can make the life fruitful. In the establishment of the kingdom some are productive and some are non-productive. Those who are productive can influence the age and generation in which they live by creating the knowledge of God, His Word and His authority. Others, alas, produce no such fruit. The wayside sowing explains the heart which has heard and never understood the Word. The beaten way of the age is hard and the Word is to such only a form, a jingle of sound. If it is snatched away from a man's heart there is no issue; no fruitfulness of any kind.

The sowing in rocky places goes farther than the first. This heart not only recognizes the Word and is familiar with it, but also rejoices in it and consents to its claims. Sadly, however, he does not allow the Word to take a grasp of his life so as to take root. When persecution and testing come in one form or another his witness fails. He then is no influence and dies away.

The sowing among thorns signifies the man who has the Word within him but who becomes so occupied with the interests of the age that the press and crush of material things, the methods, maxims, cares or pleasures of the present, so act as thorns, choking the vital principle of life that such a man becomes entirely ineffective and fruitless. The sowing in good ground indicates the heart of a man who hears, understands and responds fully to obey the voice of the King such that, in his personal life he bears fruit for the kingdom.

The Sequel

What effect are we producing upon our age and generation? The answer depends upon the extent to which the Word we know has affected our lives. What use, if we can repeat the Word, talk of it, sing of it, appear to love it and yet there is no resulting harvest in our home life, social life, business life, church life or any other life?

There are men and women in different ages and generations whose names have never appeared in newspapers who have lived in quiet obedience to the Word of their heavenly King. Angels alone may write their epitaph. They have witnessed for the King; souls have been won, hearts touched, disciples made. Let us follow in their steps and never forget that a man, woman or child won for the kingdom is the planting of a seed in our day which will result in a fuller harvest for the King.

CHAPTER FIVE: PRINCIPLES OF FORGIVENESS

THERE ARE AT LEAST three ways in which we can look at forgiveness (1) God's forgiveness of the sinner (2) the forgiveness by one forgiven sinner to another and (3) the forgiveness by a church of God of the repentant saint.

In the parable spoken by the Lord in Luke 7:40-50 we see the forgiveness of God to the sinner, and in that of Matthew 18:23-25 the forgiveness that forgiven sinners should show to one another. In the Old Testament the Holy Spirit uses three words which are translated "forgive", but one is reserved for the use of God's forgiveness only. One word has the meaning of "pardon", another the thought of "lifting" and the third the thought of "covering". In Psalm 32 David writes, "Blessed is he whose transgression (rebellion) is forgiven (lifted) whose sin (faulty action) is covered".

It is the Hebrew word 'salach', usually translated forgive or pardon which is used solely in respect of God's forgiving. When forgiveness is also shown by man the thought is that of lifting. When God appeared on the Day of Atonement in the cloud on the mercy seat which covered the Ark, the sins of the people were dealt with by God. When Paul quotes the Psalm in Romans 4:7,8 he says the iniquities were "sent away" - equivalent to "lifting" - and the sins are "covered over".

In the parable in Luke, the Lord is showing to Simon the forgiveness He extends to the sinner, even to the woman of the streets who had entered Simon's house. The simplicity of the message is contained in just fifty seven words in the Revised Version and demonstrates the simplicity of the gospel message to all who repent. No matter whether the debt is large or small the important point was that both debtors had nothing at all that they could use to pay. The debt of the thief on the cross was large - a five hundred pence debt if ever there was one, perhaps far larger than the debt of the woman whose own debt, as far as the world could judge, was larger than that of Simon. But the transcendent point was that he, Simon and the woman were completely unable to pay anything at all. The thief's only hope of forgiveness was on the basis of repentance, "death-bed" repentance though it was. All forgiveness shown by God is on the basis of the Cross and His only condition is repentance on the part of the sinner.

"Do you see this woman?" asked the Lord of Simon (NIV). He could see all right. He had probably looked at little else since she had begun her ministrations to the Lord and was thinking to himself what a poor judge of human nature he had as a guest. But he could only see the woman as she had been. The Lord saw the woman that she had become and the woman she could be when she had tasted the forgiveness that could only come with repentance. She was a fifty pence plus debtor and had nothing wherewith to pay, but now she was showing the repentance that Simon, the fifty pence debtor, never thought he needed to show.

Ephesians 1:7 speaks of "the forgiveness of our trespasses according to the riches of His grace". Thank God it is according to the riches of His grace and not our riches that forgiveness comes. The sins are sent away. "As far as the east is from the west, so far hath He removed our transgressions from us" (Psalm 103:12). We might say to each other "I can forgive but I can never forget". God not only forgives but He also forgets. The God who remembers to hold the heavens and the earth in His hands and control all things is nevertheless prepared to forget something: the fact that we had ever sinned. God was even prepared to forgive the worst crime of all - the putting to death of His Son. On the Cross the Lord could pray "Father, forgive them" and this forgiveness was shown after they had repented. Acts 6:7 tells us that "a great company of the priests were obedient to the Faith". The Lord's prayer on the Cross had been answered and the five hundred pence debtors were forgiven.

On turning to the parable in Matthew 18:23-35 we find it is much longer. In the Revised Version the number of words used is over two hundred and eighty. Why should the Lord tell another parable about forgiveness and this time have to use five times as many words as before? Because this time He is talking about the forgiveness that one man should show to another. Frail mankind finds it hard to forgive and even harder to forget. Peter had listened to the Lord speaking of forgiveness within the churches that His disciples were to establish. How many times should I forgive my brother - seven times? No, said the Lord, seventy times seven. By the time Peter had forgiven his brother that number of occasions forgiveness would have become second nature to him and he would not be able to help forgiving. Lamech in Genesis 4:24 said he would be avenged seventy seven times if anyone slighted him. But the Lord said that Peter was to show forgiveness many times more than even vicious Lamech was prepared to exact vengeance.

The parable in Matthew has unfortunately been taken out of its setting and used as an illustration of the forgiveness that the Lord shows to the sinner who is justified by faith in Christ. This is not the intention of the parable for, if so, we would have to explain how it could be that the Lord could take away the forgiveness associated with our justification. We know from other Scriptures that this would be impossible. Lose our eternal life? No. Lose the joy of salvation? Yes, that is possible, but God will never take away the forgiveness of sins that He gave to us at the new birth. No, in Matthew the Lord was dealing with human forgiveness, feeble though it is. It is noteworthy that the first two mentions of the word in the Scriptures relate to the forgiveness to be shown by men. God had certainly demonstrated His forgiving character in many ways during the whole of Genesis, but it is not until Genesis 50:17 that we get the first mention of the word. Joseph's brothers are acknowledging their sin against their brother, repenting and asking for his forgiveness. The second mention is in Exodus 10:17 where Pharaoh is asking forgiveness from Moses "only this once". His repentance was short-lived and although Moses may have been willing to forgive, God who knew the man's heart was not so prepared. In both cases the sense of the word is that of "lifting". Neither Joseph nor Moses could "cover" sins, that is, "pardon" (Hebrew - salach).

Coming back to our parable, we see that the debt forgiven by the king to the first servant was an immense fortune. How long it had been accumulating! The man must have been a very trusted servant to have been given so much credit. It was certainly beyond his ability to repay quickly, and even if the king were to put him in prison, realize all his assets and sell his family into slavery, there would still have been a huge bad debt to be written off. But notice that in this parable he would have been able to pay something. In Luke's parable the debtors had nothing at all that they could use to pay off even "a bit on account". The king moved by his pleas freely forgave him all the debt. It is here that we get the merest glimpse of the pardon that as servants we have received from the hand of God. The debt was huge but we have been freely forgiven. What should be our response? The response of the servant was to go to a fellow servant and demand repayment of his debt which amounted to a few pounds - probably equivalent to three month's wages of a labourer. It certainly could not be repaid immediately but given a reasonable amount of time and a little belt tightening here and there it could have been repaid eventually. But no. The man who had been forgiven much was not prepared to forgive less in return and would do to his debtor what the king would at first have done to him.

Notice it is his fellow servants who take action. They were appalled that so little human kindness could be shown by one who had been forgiven so much. Is this what we do when we see blatant unforgiveness being shown by a fellow-believer to another? It is matters like these that we should take to the Lord in prayer and He will act as He knows best. In this parable the king takes away the forgiveness that he showed in the first place. Is it possible that the Lord could take away what He gave to us when we came pleading forgiveness for all our sins? No, that forgiveness will never be repealed but He pleads with us, "forgiving each other ... even as the Lord forgave you" (Colossians 3:13). "And be ye kind one to another ... tender-hearted, forgiving each other, even as God also in Christ forgave you" (Ephesians 4:32).

But how does He deal with us if we don't? Mark 11:25 gives us the answer. "And whensoever ye stand praying, forgive, if ye have aught against any one; that your Father also which is in heaven may forgive you your trespasses". It is by withholding answers to our prayers that God will punish us if we do not show a forgiving spirit to others. An unforgiving spirit can become a barrier between the believer and God and lead to a powerless and prayerless life. Some Romish priests have suggested that masses paid for by the relatives of the dead can shorten the time spent in "purgatory"' and that none can come out until the last penny has been paid. That is a travesty of an interpretation of Matthew's parable. The Lord taught His disciples that when they prayed they should ask the Father, "forgive us our debts, as we also have forgiven our debtors (the Aramaic word for debt and sin are the ... For if ye forgive men their trespasses, your heavenly Father will also forgive you. But if ye forgive not men their trespasses, neither will your Father forgive your trespasses" (Matthew 6:12-15). Again, the forgiveness is to be shown before the time of prayer (see also Matthew 5:23-24) otherwise we cannot expect God to forgive the debts we owe for our daily failures. If we continue in an unforgiving spirit the barrier will always be there and we shall be the losers when our works come to be examined at the judgement seat.

CHAPTER SIX: PARABLES ABOUT PRAYER

———

WE ARE TOLD THAT IT was in the days of Enosh that men first began to call upon the Name of the Lord (Genesis 4:26). When men began to appreciate their frailty and mortality they stretched out towards the Lord in prayer.

The first specific use of the word prayer is in Genesis 20 in the matter of God's judgement on the house of Abimelech. Verse 7 is interesting in that it couples Abimelech's repentance with Abraham's prayer in the withholding of divine judgement. Thereafter throughout the Old Testament scriptures we have many examples of prayer and its effects, ranging over the lives of Moses, Hannah, Samuel, Elijah, Elisha, Hezekiah, Isaiah and others.

In seeking to learn something about prayer we are on sure ground when we come to the Gospel accounts. Here the servants have given place to the Master and in the example and words of the Lord we have rich instruction and guidance to help us in our attitude towards prayer and its practical effect in our lives.

These parables in Luke clearly present to us principles that govern requests in prayer and the divine response. In the parable in chapter 11 the response to the request was not forthcoming on the grounds of friendship. The relationship between the two friends was good. The Lord uses the same word here as He employs to describe His friends in John 15:14. A close loving friendship was not the key to success, it rather lay in an attitude of mind that would not accept "I cannot rise and give thee" for an answer.

It is, however, instructive to note that the Lord here introduces the Holy Spirit into the narrative. He is the blessed One who was to come and who dwells in our hearts. He also helpeth our infirmity: for we know not how to pray as we ought; but the Spirit Himself maketh intercession for us with groanings which cannot be uttered; and He that searcheth the hearts knoweth what is the mind of the Spirit, because He maketh intercession for the saints according to the will of God (Romans 8:26-27).

As He knows our thoughts afar off, so He also knows our needs. "Your heavenly Father knoweth that ye have need of all these things. But seek ye first His kingdom and His righteousness and all these things shall be added unto you" (Matthew 6:32-33). In all the divine ways there is balance, and we in our dealings with Him must note where the pivots lie.

In Chapter 11 verse 8 the Lord gives us an example of a man being importuned and its results. This is followed immediately by His authoritative word, "I say unto you"; directing us to Himself and to the divine response to fervency in our prayers. "Ask", says the Lord, and in the use of the word indicates our place as a suppliant: the lesser, in view of His place as the greater in giving. It is interesting that this same word is used by Joseph of Arimathea in Mark 15:43 when we are told that he went in boldly and craved (AV) the body of Jesus. "Seek", says the Lord, showing that there must be deep desire for what is wanted: not a superficial wish, but a constancy till the desired object is obtained.

"Knock" says the Lord: a stretching out after the Lord in prayer, a bridging of the gap between earth and heaven that leads to what John saw: "a door opened in heaven". It is the privilege of prayer: access to the presence of the Lord at all times and under all circumstances through that blessed One who said "I am the Way, and the Truth, and the Life, no one cometh unto the Father but by Me" (John 14:6).

The parable presented to us in chapter 18:1-7 is placed between verses which allude to the coming of the Son of Man. A waiting period is always a difficult period, trying to both patience and hope. This parable is a strong encouragement to continue steadfastly in prayer (Acts 2:42). The operative word in Luke 18:1 is "always". In considering this parable and its object it is an interesting study to lay it alongside Isaiah 40:27-31. Note that the One who "fainteth not" gives power to the faint and those who wait upon the Lord will renew their strength and not faint.

It was unfortunate for the woman in the parable that she was dealing with an unrighteous judge. It was only her persistence and a wearing down of the judge that won her the day. Proverbs 21:3 tells us "To do justice and judgement is more acceptable to the LORD than sacrifice". Elijah prayed fervently and he prayed again (James 5:17-18). The believer prays again and again and again to a righteous God who will respond according to a standard of righteousness and knowledge that is eternal and impartial. It is interesting to note that the Lord draws our attention to the words of an unrighteous man for our guidance. In some cases the sons of this world are for their own generation wiser than the sons of the light (Luke 16:8).

There is a lovely expression in verse 7: "His elect", showing that deep relationship between the Lord and His own, and His deep interest in them and in their prayers. This verse is of further interest in that it underlines an aspect of the divine character - God is patient with His own and shows great patience with their prayers. He is a long-suffering God who, when the time comes to act, will do so swiftly and decisively. The example has been set. We too must show patience when looking for an answer to our prayers. The words of David and Jeremiah are relevant in the context of the foregoing. "I waited patiently for the LORD; and He inclined unto me and heard my cry" (Psalm 40:1) and "It is good that a man should hope and quietly wait for the salvation of the LORD" (Lamentations 3:26).

In our last parable in verses 9-14 we are clearly taught principles of humility and condition which should govern our prayer life. The Lord had specific persons in mind when He told this parable. The One who knows the heart and the mind of all men directs these words to "certain which trusted in themselves that they were righteous, and set all others at nought"; a dangerous and unbecoming state of mind for any man to be in.

The two men went to the right place - the Place of the Name and the place of the altar. "O Thou that hearest prayer, unto Thee shall all flesh come" (Psalm 65:2), and "My house shall be a house of prayer" (Luke 19:46). The Pharisee went with pride in his heart and a high look in his eyes. "An high look, and a proud heart, even the lamp of the wicked is sin" (Proverbs 21:4). We are told that he prayed thus with himself. Foolish man, to speak about himself to himself, self-sufficient man with no sense of sin or the deep needs of his soul, with no humility or awe as he approached his God. He was a man who asked nothing for himself and had no place in his prayer for others; a man who in his own estimation was unique - "not as the rest of men" - forgetting that all have sinned and that all our righteousnesses are as filthy rags in His sight.

What a contrast is seen in the publican, who knew he was in the far off place and took that place in his approach to God, bringing no self-justification and offering nothing in self-commendation. His eyes were not upward as were the Pharisee's but directed perhaps to the altar where the sacrifice lay - the great ground of mercy and propitiation. He smote his breast, knowing that the trouble lay within, and took the sinner's place. Few words came from the depths of his soul: "God, he merciful to me a sinner".

The Lord here exercises His authority and arbitrates between these two men. Note the "I say unto you" of verse 14. The Judge of all the earth gives His verdict, and the publican who came with humility returns to his house a justified man. Paul said, "For this cause I bow my knees unto the Father" (Ephesians 3:14). It is a lovely experience to bow ourselves in the presence of God, to recognize His greatness and omnipotence, to confess that He is Lord of all and that all our fountains are in Him (Psalm 87:7). To confess our unworthiness and to be like Jacob who recognized that he was "not worthy of the least of all the mercies, and of all the truth which Thou hast shewed unto Thy servant" (Genesis 32:10) will be to receive the blessing that comes to those of a contrite and humble spirit (Isaiah 57:15).

CHAPTER SEVEN: PERISHABLE RICHES

"THE WORLD'S WEALTH and morality are in constant tension": these words come from a recent report entitled "The root of all evil?" and confirm that little has changed since the Lord Jesus Christ used parables to drive home the same message. The parables of Luke chapters 12 and 16 form part of the Lord's ministry during His last journey to Jerusalem. In Luke 12 He was referring to the omnipotence of God and of man's dependence on Him when He was interrupted by a man preoccupied with his brother's injustice over his part of their inheritance. God's Son speaks of divine things, yet this man, blind to the significance of the occasion and able to think only of money, blurts out his problem and demands arbitration. His insensitivity brings no direct rebuke, but the telling parable of the rich farmer who saw nothing beyond material things.

Luke 12: The Dangers of Wealth

Scripture does not regard wealth as intrinsically evil, but rather a blessing from God (Psalm 112:1-3; Ecclesiastes 5:19); wealth not only bestows great power but also brings comparable dangers and obligations. The rich farmer of the parable was able to provide for himself a life of retired ease and comfort. The purpose of the story, and it must have driven deep into the man with the money problem, is to point out the folly of omitting God from the reckoning. The farmer trusted in riches and his own foresight and planning (note the repeated use of the personal pronoun in vv. 17-19) to the exclusion of the things of God. In Mark 10:17-27 the Lord further stresses the problems of riches, and the disciples were quick to grasp that these problems beset us all.

The farmer had fallen prey to materialism in the mistaken belief that present wealth is all-important, forgetting that true riches are laid up in heaven (see also 2 Corinthians 4:16-18). Covetousness - the envious desire for riches - is ever the close ally of materialism. The Christian today is no less exposed to the dangers of wealth and the lure of riches. Israel long ago were warned of these same dangers (Deuteronomy 8:11-20) and the Lord's words have not diminished in their relevance to ourselves and to our acquisitive, materialist age. John, writing to the Church in Laodicea, gives the Lord's assessment of them: "Because thou sayest, I am rich, and have gotten riches, and have need of nothing; and knowest not that thou art the wretched one and miserable and poor and blind and naked: I counsel thee to buy of Me gold refined by fire, that thou mayest become rich" (Revelation 3:17-18). The Laodicean Christians, like the rich farmer, were materially affluent yet were bankrupt toward God who assesses true wealth.

Are riches, then, incompatible with the disciple's life? The Lord said in the parable of the sower that the seed sown among thorns "is he that heareth the Word; and the care of the world, and the deceitfulness of riches, choke the Word, and he becometh unfruitful" (Matthew 13:22). It could hardly be more clearly stated. Although it may be possible to have and correctly to handle wealth, the dangers are such that, in general, riches tend to deaden rather than encourage faith in and dependence upon God because pride in human ability is so much involved. Riches are ever liable to cheat a man so that his life becomes unfruitful so far as God is concerned simply because "where your treasure is, there will your heart be also" (Luke 12:34).

Paul develops the theme in 1 Timothy 6:9-10, stating that the love of money is a root of all kinds of evil: which some reaching after have been led away from the Faith, and have pierced themselves through with many sorrows. The antithesis of the anxiety and sorrow that so often spring from materialism is the contentment that derives from a deep reliance on God.

The Lord, in Luke 12:22-34, follows the parable of the farmer with a word to His disciples about contentment and a reminder that God has an especial care for those who are His. In Luke 3:14 soldiers were told by John the Baptist to be content with their wages and the instruction in Hebrews 13:5 is: "be ye 'free from the love of money; content with such things as ye have: for Himself hath said, I will in no wise fail thee, neither will I in any wise forsake thee".

This principle, expounded in its fulness in the New Testament, is nevertheless of great antiquity. David said in Psalm 62:10 "if riches increase, set not your heart thereon" and Job, having learned to trust despite having lost all his possessions, his health, and most of his family, found that God was able to give him more than he had originally. Paul spoke from the depth of his personal experience when he told the Philippians, "I have learned, in whatsoever state I am, therein to be content. I know how to be abased, and I know also how to abound: in everything and in all things have I learned the secret both to be filled and to be hungry, both to abound and to be in want" (Philippians 4:11-12).

In these few words he expresses the outcome of a profound process of learning the ways of God that the Lord Himself expounded: to be independent of either poverty or wealth, to be in bondage to neither. Paul goes further, and explains how this can be: "I can do all things in Him that strengtheneth me" (Philippians 4:13); he trusted God to supply his needs, and this is the practical application of the Lord's word to the disciples in Luke 12. We may readily assent to this, but to how many of us is it a practical reality?

Luke 16: The Obligations of Wealth

Here the Lord tells the disciples of the unjust steward - a plausible, unscrupulous rogue who, having miscalculated, and knowing that he would be called to task for his misdeeds, was nevertheless sufficiently shrewd to secure his advantage. The Lord does not commend him, but uses the story to jolt His hearers and to teach them that His followers are expected to manage their affairs with prudence. Wealth brings great responsibilities. The word mammon, used only in Matthew 6:24 and Luke 16:9, 11 and 13, is the transliteration of the Aramaic word for wealth or profit. In Matthew 6 the Lord regards mammon as that obsessive covetousness that consumes a man and can so easily estrange him from God, and it is in this context that He said "Ye cannot serve God and mammon" (v.24), thereby exposing the hypocrisy of the Pharisees who loved money and scoffed at His words (Luke 16:14).

He next relates the parable of the rich man and Lazarus to show that the present is the time to practise the longstanding biblical principle of caring for the disadvantaged. The rich man lived well, indifferent to the dire need of Lazarus. This principle of using wealth, not for personal satisfaction, but before God to the benefit of others, necessarily implies that some, at least must be relatively affluent. The parable of the good Samaritan (Luke 10:30-37) carries the Lord's approval of the caring attitude that should characterize His followers.

The key to the proper discharge of the obligations brought by wealth is the recognition that the disciple is not the absolute owner of the wealth that God has given and hence is not free to use it selfishly, but is instead a steward who is accountable to his Lord for the faithful and wise use of that which has been entrusted to him (see 1 Corinthians 4:2). Once again, it is Paul who further expounds the principle in 1 Timothy 6:17-19. The rich are told to do good, and to be ready to distribute and communicate. He commends in 2 Corinthians 8 and 9 the way in which this principle was expressed in the early churches of God in Macedonia by saints who gave themselves and their substance in the service of God.

In so doing these disciples were emulating in a practical way the ultimate sacrifice of the Lord Jesus Christ who "though He was rich, yet for your sakes He became poor, that ye through His poverty might become rich" (2 Corinthians 8:9), thereby laying up for themselves the true riches - treasure in heaven - of which the Lord spoke (see 2 Corinthians 9:6-15).

The acquisition of wealth and the wealth-creation process also raise moral questions, for wealth can be gained by honest endeavour or by less honourable means. The Christian is told to work heartily and to live honestly (Colossians 3:23-24; 1 Thessalonians 4:11-12; Hebrews 13:18), leaving the matter of reward to God. Tainted money, obtained other than by honest means, has no part in the service of a holy and righteous God. Judas Iscariot is a stark example of a disciple whose life was blighted by the love of money. He was, presumably, with the other disciples and heard the Lord's teaching concerning money and material wealth yet by this time, he had so come to love it that he is described as a thief (John 12:46).

Eventually his whole being was taken over and he stooped to betray the Lord for the paltry sum of thirty pieces of silver. But Judas, seeing the outcome of his greed and treachery, was unable to keep the money and, having been smitten with remorse, only to be so contemptuously spurned by his paymasters, flings it away in the temple and takes his life. The erstwhile disciple had become the son of perdition (John 17:12). What could be in more marked contrast to the Lord's words: "lay up for yourselves treasures in heaven, where neither moth nor rust doth consume, and where thieves do not break through and steal: for where thy treasure is, there will thy heart be also" (Matthew 6:20-21)? These eternal treasures are wealth indeed.

CHAPTER EIGHT: FAITHFUL AND UNFAITHFUL SERVANTS

THE TITLE OF THIS CHAPTER sets forth a distinction that will be made by the Lord among those who have sought to serve Him while here on earth. There can be little doubt as to what commendation a servant of Christ would wish to have written over his or her service at its conclusion; surely all would wish to hear the Master say: "Well done, good and faithful servant" (Matthew 25:21).

When the time comes for the Lord to pronounce His assessment of each of His servants, it will be for some a time of regret and perhaps remorse. In order to avoid loss at the divine appraisal, what qualities should mark the servants of Christ during their time of service? The answer to this question is enshrined in our Lord's teaching, particularly His parables. We shall now consider three parables that illustrate a number of desirable qualities.

Luke 12:35-48: Preparedness

The setting of this parable is the time of the coming of the Son of Man (12:40), when Christ will return to earth to judge and to reign. However, the main principles set out in the parable are applicable where and whenever there is a waiting people.

From the early days of this dispensation, believers have been taught to expect the imminent return of Christ. One of the earlier New Testament writings takes up the matter of the Lord's return (1 Thessalonians 4:13-18). Also in one of the latest New Testament books, the subject of Christ's coming is again dealt with (1 John 2:28). If believers in apostolic times looked for the Lord's return in their day, how much more must we, who are almost two thousand years closer to the event, be looking for its imminent fulfilment?

The fact that the Lord has chosen not to reveal the exact date of His return should engender in His servants a constant sense of expectancy and with it a continuous state of preparedness. This is the main thrust of the parable, taking emphasis from our Lord's words in vv.39,40. Such an air of expectancy should manifest itself in continual preparatory activities. The parable opens with a scene depicting people maintaining themselves in a state of constant preparation: "Let your loins be girded about and your lamps burning" (v.35). It is ours as a waiting people today, to be ever active in our spiritual service, thus being always ready for our Lord's return.

Peter's question: "Lord, speakest Thou this parable unto us, or even unto all?" (v.41) is an interesting one. Was this parable to have a limited application to Jesus' disciples only, or was it to apply to all in the multitude who listened to His words? A comparison with Mark 13:37 would suggest that the wider application was intended. Since it is set in the days of the coming of the Son of Man, the parable would be applicable to those of Israel who are looking for the coming of the Messiah and to believing Gentiles who are expecting His return as Son of Man.

Some find difficulty with the punishments meted out to servants in vv. 46-48. We should remember, however, that we are dealing with a parable and the point at issue is that of relative accountability. The key to this passage is found in the words: "And to whomsoever much is given, of him shall much be required; and to whom they commit much, of him will they ask the more" (v.48). Servants of Christ will be judged by Him according to their spiritual understanding and gift. If those who are greatly enlightened and gifted by the Lord fail to exercise these attributes to His glory, then they will suffer greater shame and loss at the judgement seat of Christ than those less favoured than themselves.

Luke 16: 1-13: Righteousness

The parable of the unrighteous steward has been the subject of various interpretations down through the years since its telling. It is therefore useful to keep the following points in mind: (a) In this parable, the Lord's teaching method is to present the antithesis of the qualities He desires to be seen in His followers, highlighting them by contrast. (b) In vv. 10-13 Christ explains the moral of the parable, and the narrative should he interpreted in the light of His words. (c) From Luke 15:11 to 16:31 the Lord relates three incidents; the prodigal son, the unrighteous steward and the rich man and Lazarus, in which among other things, He puts earthly riches into their true perspective.

In vv.10-13 Christ details three things that He desires His disciples to be faithful, righteous and single hearted. Faithfulness is the quality of keeping faith with, or remaining true to, a person, an ideal, a task or responsibility. This is a characteristic that was lacking in the steward of the parable, for accusations reached his employer's ear that the steward was not remaining true to his duty of administering his master's estate to profit' but was rather wasting his goods (v.1). In 1 Corinthians 4:2, Paul views his service for Christ as a ministry or stewardship, and the thing that he desires to be the hallmark of his stewardship is faithfulness. Paul, the faithful steward, could examine his own conscience and say truly: "For I know nothing against myself" (1 Corinthians 4:4). Can we say the same?

The unfaithful conduct of the steward in the parable sprang from his lack of personal righteousness. He was obviously a man without scruple, for his action in reducing the amount of the debts owed to his master (vv. 5-7) indicates that he was prepared to use the authority given to him by his master to further his own ends. A person's faithfulness and righteousness, or lack of it, will be indicated in the relatively unimportant things, and what is characteristic in unimportant matters, will be true in the larger sphere; this thought is the essence of v.10. The unrighteous mammon, the money and goods of this life, is the relatively unimportant sphere in which can be seen a person's true character, whether he is righteous or not. If we as servants of Christ also bear in mind that what we have in the way of possessions is in the final analysis what has been given us by God, then we must accept that we are responsible for that which is another's (cf. v.12). Thus in our actions and attitudes concerning material things can be seen characteristics good or bad, which will be evident in the more important sphere of spiritual service.

So often this matter of attitude towards material riches is the point at which many fail to make spiritual progress, like the rich young man of Matthew 19:16-22. Or just as tragically those who are going on well in spiritual stewardship are turned aside by the siren song of material gain and find their spiritual lives dashed upon the rocks of worldliness. Paul in his observations of just such dangers says: "But they that desire to be rich fall into a temptation ... the love of money ... which some reaching after have been led astray from the Faith, and have pierced themselves through with many sorrows" (1 Timothy 6:9,10).

The quality of singleness of heart is touched upon in v.13 of the parable. The Lord warns that, "No servant can serve two masters", for his loyalty would then be divided and a conflict of interest set up. Again Christ warns that pursuing material gain is a likely cause of such a conflict: "Ye cannot serve: God and mammon". Paul, in illustrating this matter of single-heartedness, takes up the analogy of the soldier: "No soldier on service entangleth himself in the affairs of this life; that he may please him who enrolled him as a soldier" (2 Timothy 2:4).

Verses 8 and 9 of this parable need careful thought for the Lord would at first glance appear to be commending the shady business practice of the unrighteous steward; this of course cannot be so. In verse 8 we are told that the master of the steward commended his action and Jesus then explains why the action was viewed as wise: "For the sons of this world are for their own generation wiser than the sons of the light". That is to say, viewing things from the perspective of this life only, worldly men are more prudent in providing for their material well-being than the sons of light. But when the longer view of eternity is taken into account then short term material gain will be shown to be a poor substitute for true riches. In light of this, our Lord's words in verse 9 are perhaps in the nature of an irony; for how can friends whose actions are motivated by unrighteous mammon be of any value as to the eternal tabernacles?

Luke 17: 7-10: Subjection

To the uncommitted onlooker it may seem that in the qualities asked of the disciple of Christ, there is something in the nature of a burdensome task, and the natural man rebels at the thought of having to put his shoulder to such a burden. Not only unbelieving men of the world, but children of God also at times seek to shirk their responsibility to follow the disciple pathway and serve the whole counsel of God. This "Will I/ Won't I?" question, turns on the attitude of heart within the believer. Is the attitude to be that of choosing to serve one's own ends or, in subjection and obedience, to serve the purposes of the Master?

In this matter of fixing the attitude of heart, the Lord Jesus directs the thoughts of the disciples to the natural relationship between earthly servant and master. He asks them to consider what their own attitude towards a bondservant would be, if they were in the position of masters (v.7). Would their outlook not be that it is the servant's place to serve the master, not the other way round, and that no special thanks were due to a servant who simply did that which was expected of him (vv. 8-9)?

These things being so, the attitude of the servants of Christ should be acceptance of their position as servants, and a humble subjection to that which is expected of them, counting it as no more than their duty (v.10).

Although the attitude of the master in this parable would be the expected norm; it does not follow that it mirrors the attitude of our gracious Master. Indeed, from Luke 12:37, 38 it would appear that the opposite will be true. To those who display the characteristics of preparedness, faithfulness, righteousness, single heartedness and subjection will come the words of praise with which we began this article and which will have eternal import: "Well done good and faithful servant".

CHAPTER NINE: TALENTS AND POUNDS

THE PARABLES OF THE talents and the pounds both refer primarily to the Lord's return to the earth as Son of Man when He will subdue His enemies and set up His world-wide kingdom. In this context the references to the unprofitable servant being cast into outer darkness in the parable of the talents, and to the enemies being slain in the parable of the pounds are easily understood, for that is precisely what will happen when the Lord comes to reign. However, in this article we wish to draw out some principles of service and reward which are applicable today to disciples of the Lord Jesus.

There is not the slightest doubt that the parables have their application to us also, for the nobleman who went into a far country to receive a kingdom and to return is our Lord and Master, whose return we also await, and when He comes we shall appear before His judgement seat to give account of our service. "Trade ye herewith till I come" is clearly His word to our hearts also, and it places upon us all a tremendous responsibility to serve Him with all the strength and zeal we can muster until we hear the call "Behold, He cometh". Let us learn then by comparison and contrast the lessons touching our service for the Lord which these parables teach, and we shall do so under three headings. Firstly:

The Stewardship Entrusted to Them

In both parables bondservants are involved and we remember the apostle Paul loved to describe himself in that way - "Paul, a bondservant of Jesus Christ" (Romans 1:1). What we write has particular application to those who have yielded their hearts to Him, and who no longer live unto themselves but unto Him who for their sakes died and rose again.

In the first parable three servants are mentioned and the gifts of five, two and one talents were varied according to their several ability. Our minds turn immediately to the spiritual gifts which our ascended Master gave, "gifts differing according to the grace that was given to us" (Romans 12:6). The apostle Paul made it clear "there are diversities of gifts, but the same Spirit", for He divides "to each one severally even as He will" (1 Corinthians 12:4,11). And the apostle Peter adds to our understanding of the subject when he says "according as each hath received a gift, ministering it among yourselves" (1 Peter 4:10). "To each one" is a phrase often repeated in connection with spiritual gifts and it emphasizes the fact that no member of the Church, which is His Body is left out. Each has received a gift as an endowment for service and we are responsible to use it until He comes.

In the second parable there were ten servants and each received a pound. Once again it was to be used in service, but this time it was the same value to each one. Our minds reflect on the Master's words, just before He died, "I have given them Thy Word; and the world hated them" (John 17:14). It is interesting how He places the two facts together, the giving of His Word and the hatred of the world. It answers to the parable, for those ten servants lived and laboured in a hostile environment among citizens who hated their absent lord. We find ourselves in similar circumstances, serving in a world which has no time for the Master we love. But He has given us God's Word; to each one of us the same precious and powerful Word of God which the world so desperately needs. With it we are to serve as workmen and if we handle it rightly we shall not need to be ashamed.

The apostle Paul wrote of elders who laboured in the Word and in teaching (1 Timothy 5:17) and the Greek word conveys the thought of labouring with wearisome effort. They put all they had into it, and so must we. Whatever spiritual gift we have been given, whether teacher, pastor or evangelist; whether we give ourselves to ministry, teaching or exhortation, we shall find they each stand related to the Word of God. The man of God is furnished completely unto every good work by the precious deposit of the Sacred Writings. And even if we consider what we might think of as the lesser gifts we shall find that they also require that we handle God's Word. As the pounds increased as they were used, so will God's Word. It did in apostolic days. "The Word of God increased" (Acts 6:7), "grew and multiplied" (12:24), "so mightily grew the Word of the Lord and prevailed" (19:20). We turn now to consider as our second point:

The Response of the Servants

They did not serve with their own resources. Each of them served with what they had received. It was a stewardship entrusted to them and "it is required in stewards, that a man be found faithful" (1 Corinthians 4:2). Not surprisingly, therefore, faithfulness is highlighted in both parables. In the parable of the talents the lord's word was "Well done, good and faithful servant: thou hast been faithful over a few things, I will set thee over many things". In the parable of the pounds, there are similar words of commendation and a reference to having been found faithful. We are forcibly reminded that God does not expect us to do more than we are able, but serve faithfully with the talents we are given. Paul's words in a slightly different context are nevertheless applicable that "if the readiness is there, it is acceptable according as a man hath, not according as he hath not" (2 Corinthians 8:12). The servant with the two talents did not concern himself with the fact that his fellow-servant was entrusted with five. In his lord's estimation he had ability to serve with two talents and he faithfully worked away until his two had grown to four.

However, in both parables there was one servant who failed. The 'one talent man' hid his talent in the earth, and the one with the pound wrapped it in a napkin. A gift lay unused and therefore unproductive, and it turns our thoughts to Paul's word to Timothy, "Neglect not the gift that is in thee" (1 Timothy 4:14) and later "stir up the gift of God, which is in thee" (2 Timothy 1:6). We each have a gift and we do well to examine ourselves regarding it. Are we using it diligently or would we in any way come under the condemnation of the slothful servant? "In diligence not slothful; fervent in spirit; serving the Lord" is the apostle's instruction immediately following his teaching about the gifts in Romans 12.

The Day of Reckoning

The Day of Reckoning is coming and this is our third point. We are accountable for what we have received. "Each one of us shall give account of himself to God" (Romans 14:12). It will be a verbal account, for at the judgement seat of Christ we shall each be required to speak. In both parables the lord or nobleman returned as he had said he would and at his command his servants stood before him. It was a solemn time, of praise and reward for those who had proved faithful, but of loss for the one unfaithful. The contemplation of it causes us to search our hearts, for our Master also has gone away and will return. "If I go ... I come again "He said, and about that we have no doubt. But how shall we meet Him when He comes? Will it be with joy or shall we be ashamed before Him at His coming?

"I have gained other five talents" said one of the servants. "Lord, thy pound hath made ten pounds more" said another. There were two ways of viewing it: "I laboured more abundantly than they all" wrote the apostle Paul, "yet not I, but the grace of God which was with me" (1 Corinthians 15:10). We recall that grace was given according to the gift. Happy shall we be in that day if we can say, "His grace which was bestowed upon me was not found vain".

The day of reckoning is coming. In both parables the reward for faithful service was authority in his coming kingdom. Because "thou hast been faithful in a few things, I will set thee over many things" (Matthew 25:21,23). "Because thou hast been faithful in a very little, have thou authority over ten cities ... five cities" (Luke 19:17,19). "Know ye not that the saints shall judge the world?" (1 Corinthians 6:2) asked the apostle Paul. "If we endure, we shall also reign with Him" (2 Timothy 2:12). Glorious prospect! But perhaps more precious than all will be to hear Him say "Well done, good and faithful servant ... enter thou into the joy of thy Lord". Is there anything we would desire more, than that by our life and service we might bring Him joy?

CHAPTER TEN: THE VINEYARD AND THE FIG TREE

NO DOUBT SOME OF YOU have looked down with satisfaction on a basket of delicious fruit after a "pick your own" session at a fruit farm. Hopefully, the owner, who provided every facility, enjoyed a good return on his investment also. That's how things should be, isn't it? Sadly, acts of criminal violence, or crop failure, for example, can sometimes ruin a promising harvest. Then the owner is denied his rightful return and we come home empty handed. The two parables we now consider deal with such matters, emphasizing crucial spiritual lessons for both the individual and the people of God.

The parable of the vineyard and the wicked tenants - recorded in Matthew 21:33-46 as well as in Mark and Luke - was prophetically delivered by the Lord to the Jewish leaders just a few days before they crucified Him. It contains a most vivid illustration of a nation's persistent rejection of God and its consequences for them. But it also provides the first public and supremely important announcement of an imminent new order which the Lord had earlier promised His disciples.

Every Facility Provided

Scripture had declared, "The vineyard of the LORD ... is the house of Israel" (Isaiah 5:7), and our Lord's graphic description of a first class vineyard is almost an echo of the one His Spirit had moved Isaiah to give over seven hundred years earlier. Then, the "Well beloved" had similarly provided every facility, yet sadly, the vineyard only produced wild grapes. "What could have been done more to My vineyard, that I have not done in it?" He asked disappointedly, and then with sorrow He had to announce, "I will lay it waste" (Isaiah 5:1-6).

We recall that in the parable the many servants of the patient vineyard owner, sent to collect his proceeds, were rejected and violently abused, even to the extent of murder. And so the story was Israel's story. Richly provided for and brought into divine inheritance, the people grew increasingly indifferent to their privileges and their Provider, although often He sent His prophets to them "rising up early ... because He had compassion on His people". But to their shame, indifference degenerated into rejection - "They mocked the messengers of God, and despised His words, and scoffed at His prophets" (2 Chronicles 36:15,16).

The Levites' prayer of Nehemiah 9 so accurately summarizes Israel's tragic decline from halcyon days of valued riches to the darkest days of violent rejection. From "all good things" to the time when "they were disobedient ... and slew Thy prophets which testified against them" (vv. 24-26). How fearful to contemplate that God's people could sink so low! And how it must have broken our Saviour's tender heart to recall their history as He cried, "O Jerusalem, Jerusalem, which killeth the prophets, and stoneth them that are sent unto her! How often would I have gathered thy children together ... and ye would not!" (Matthew 23:37).

What Shall I Do?

The long-suffering vineyard owner, faced with such gross abuse and rejection, pondered hard as to what he could do to recover his rightful possession. Luke tells us he asked, "What shall I do?" An indication to us on the human level that it was no light thing for Almighty God in His eternal counsels to ensure the recovery of that of which sin had robbed Him. In Mark's account we read, "Having yet therefore one son, his well beloved, he sent him also last unto them, saying, 'They will reverence my son'" (Mark 12:6 KJV). What words to contemplate! His servants had been rejected, what could he do? He had the means to arrange for the wicked tenants to be destroyed, but he also had one very precious son whom he loved dearly and for whom he had great plans. It would break this father's heart to lose him, but surely, he thought, they would respect his only son and heir. So the patient man decided to give the wretches a last chance; hoping for the best, yet risking his dearest, he sent his beloved son. In devoted obedience and with great courage, the young man made the fateful journey which, alas, took him to his violent death.

With what pathos the Master Narrator presents the truth about Himself! The truth which is perceived by both comparison and contrast: He "the Only Begotten from the Father" was the One whom the Father sanctified and sent into the world (John 10:36). Then, in contrast to those in the parable, Father and Son knew every detail of the worst that man would do. But in spite of the awful cost, and because there was no other way, last of all the Well beloved was freely given. And so the One who, above all others, should have been reverenced by Israel, was despised and rejected. They cast Him out of the vineyard too, and outside the gate He suffered and died at their hands.

Kingdom Rejected

Remarkably, the consequences of their action were described by the elders themselves in response to the Lord's question. The vineyard owner would "miserably destroy those miserable men" and would "let out the vineyard unto other husbandmen". There is an urgent warning here for individuals who reject Christ; for they too will suffer destruction, eternal destruction. How solemn! May we be prayerfully concerned that many will be saved from this.

Now as far as the nation of Israel is concerned, because they rejected the Son, who was indeed their King, they did in consequence reject His kingdom too. Though they would carry on their formal religion, until their future restoration, it would become empty void of the privileges of the kingdom of God. How very sad! In describing their religious activity, the Lord changed the illustration to that of builders when He reminded them of the solemn prediction of Psalm 118:22, "The Stone which the builders rejected, the same was made the Head of the corner". Though He was vital to them, they had no place for Him in their projects. So what had been God's house, became their "desolate" house. In contrast, the rejected Stone would become the chief Corner Stone of a new structure for God, to be built by another nation.

The Lord had earlier made a most precious promise to His disciples when He said, "Fear not, little Flock; for it is your Father's good pleasure to give you the kingdom" (Luke 12:32). Later, during forty days following His resurrection, He spoke to them "the things concerning the kingdom of God" (Acts 1:3), and instructed the apostles to teach others all that He had commanded. Thus the new phase of the kingdom of God, introduced and explained by the Lord Himself, came to have its written constitution when His teaching became enshrined in the apostles' writings, as directed by the promised Holy Spirit:

Today's Privilege

Briefly, let us consider two such writings; firstly, Peter's first epistle to the dispersed Jewish believers In chapter 2 verses 4-10 he also quotes the passage from Psalm 118, and points out that they had come to Christ the chief Corner Stone, and as living stones themselves, were "built up a spiritual house ... a holy nation, a people for God's own possession which in time past were no people, but now are the people of God". What a privilege is ours in the later part of this same dispensation of grace to be built together into the spiritual house; to enjoy this supreme national status we who were nobodies! But do we value our divine status and privileges as highly as we should?

The other passage we would briefly refer to is Romans chapters 9 to 11: the apostle Paul's exposition of aspects of the profound doctrine of election. Paramount in his argument are two issues; on the one hand, the fall of the Jewish nation in ceasing to be the people of God because of their disobedience; and on the other hand, salvation and divine nationhood becoming available to the Gentiles. And in keeping with our parable of the vineyard the apostle points out that we, believing Gentiles, were grafted in. Should we not, each one of us therefore, bow in awe and gratitude at this thought, "Branches were broken off, that I might be grafted in"? (Romans 11:19) May God help us truly to appreciate our position today.

As we conclude our consideration of the parable of the vineyard we are reminded of that telling phrase, "bringing forth the fruits thereof" (Matthew 21:43) descriptive of God's purpose for His holy nation. Tragically, that purpose was constantly frustrated and finally dashed, as far as Israel was concerned, when the Son of God was Slain. In contrast, in our second parable (the Fig Tree, Luke 13:6-9), the vineyard owner came three years in succession seeking fruit, but met no hostility or violence - just a barren tree. It was a waste of valuable space, yet patiently he gave the vinedresser one more year to tend the tree that it might, at last, produce the intended fruit: If not, then it would have to be destroyed.

Today's Danger

Significantly, we are not told the outcome in the second parable, but clearly we are expected to heed the danger and warning. The people of God of our generation may not be guilty of the violent rejection of God's Son, illustrated by the first parable; but sadly, we could very easily, through worldliness and materialism, for example, become indifferent and cold-hearted, with the resultant barrenness - the absence of the fruit of the Spirit in our lives, individual and collective. And in this respect we recall that the Ephesian saints were warned that unless they repented, God would remove their lampstand. So in our own day, while we can rejoice in the security of our souls, we tremble lest our status as God's holy nation be forfeited.

May each one of us therefore respond to these parables with sentiments such as the following: "The great vineyard Owner was willing to send His only beloved Son, to be despised, rejected and slain; not only that I might be saved from Hell, but also be purchased as part of a people for His own possession, zealous of good works (Titus 2:14). May I never be indifferent to such precious knowledge."

CHAPTER ELEVEN: THE MARRIAGE FEAST AND THE GREAT SUPPER

ALTHOUGH PARABLES WERE the means the Lord Jesus used to describe the kingdom of heaven so as to conceal its meaning from the Pharisees and other Jewish leaders (Matthew 13:11-13), they were in no doubt that He was speaking about them. This had the effect of merely intensifying their opposition to Him (Matthew 21:45-46). He began these parables, as recorded in the 13th chapter of Matthew, as a consequence of their clear rejection of Him and His unambiguous message to them: "repent ye; for the kingdom of heaven is at hand". This chapter thus makes a turning point in His presentation to the nation of Israel.

The Marriage Feast

The parable that we are considering is in chapter 22 of Matthew. It is the parable of the king's marriage feast for his son, one of many parables in Matthew's gospel. It looks forward to that great future occasion when God the Father will honour His Son, the Lamb who was slain, at His union with His bride, for whom He gave Himself. This event is described in Revelation 19:6-9, where it says: "Blessed are they which are bidden to the marriage supper of the Lamb". What an honour to be invited, and what an honour to be there in His presence at that time - to eat and drink with Him in that future kingdom and to behold His glory which His Father has given Him (John 17:24). And how much greater it will be than that simple wedding feast, in Cana, at which His disciples first saw His glory (John 2:11).

Rejection and Substitution

The central theme of this parable is the rejection of the invitation to the feast: The guests had been individually chosen beforehand, then summoned when the king was ready to receive them, but they would not come. No rejection by men can ever forestall the purposes of God, which are from everlasting: the marriage feast must proceed, the son, the heir, must be honoured. And so other guests must be found. We see working here God's principle of substitution of blessing. He will not force the hearts of men; others will be invited until the place of blessing is filled. This is reminiscent of Israel's earlier history when a whole generation would not enter into Canaan under Moses' leadership in response to the call of God. But God's purpose of having His people in their promised land could not be frustrated on that occasion either. He waited for the following generation, for those who would be willing to go in, this time under Joshua's leadership. It was with them, not their parents, that His purpose was fulfilled.

This is a solemn warning to all of us that our blessings and rewards from God can be forfeited to another because of a lack of obedience and response to the Word of God. God intends our blessing, but not at the cost of His own purpose and glory; that is pre-eminent:

The Great Supper

In Luke chapter 14, there is an account of a different, but somewhat similar, supper. Again the original invitations were spurned and so others were invited. The Lord told this to Pharisees and lawyers with whom He was eating, in response to a statement by one of them that seemed to presume that they were the ones who would enjoy the privilege of eating in the future kingdom of God. Both of these passages refer to the casting away, for a time, of Israel as a nation because of the hardening of their hearts, as Romans 11 describes. It is this casting away that has provided to Gentiles the opportunity of salvation (Romans 11:11,12,15,25).

Invitations to the Marriage Feast

In Matthew's parable, which pertains to the kingdom of heaven, there were three distinct invitations, with varying responses. The first, to the chosen guests, portrays the preaching of the Old Testament prophets to Israel about the coming Messiah. When Jesus came as that Messiah, He proclaimed that the kingdom of heaven was "at hand". This was the time for those invited guests to come to' Him, and John the Baptist and the Lord's own apostles and others summoned Israel to Him. This was the second invitation. The reaction by some was indifference, but by some was violence. The servants, John, Stephen and the apostle James were killed. Others, such as Peter, were imprisoned and many suffered persecution. Israel's leaders were found "not worthy" of the marriage feast and so were set aside.

Then a third invitation was sent out: This time the servants were sent with a wide open invitation, to "whosoever will", to the highways outside the city. This was no longer an appeal to the nation but a personal invitation, to bad and good alike, without distinction. This was the Lord's own appeal to the common Jewish people: "Come unto Me, all ye that labour and are heavy laden" (Matthew 11:28), many of whom believed on Him. He had said "Blessed are the poor in spirit; for theirs is the kingdom of heaven" (Matthew 5:3). It was also the appeal of Paul and others later to Gentiles, and it will be the appeal to all the nations when "the gospel of the kingdom" is again proclaimed prior to the second coming of the Messiah to earth (Matthew 24:14).

Invitations to the Great Supper

In Luke's account, which pertains to the kingdom of God, there were four invitations. The first three were similar to those in Matthew 22, but a fourth was added in order to fill the house. Again. the response of those specially invited guests was indifference. They all made excuses for seemingly legitimate circumstances. But they were pre-occupied with their present occupations - their property, their business, their personal relationships - things which can be "weights" that encumber us, as Hebrews 12:1 describes them. They were clearly not waiting expectantly for the summons to the great supper to which they had previously been invited. And so, when it came, they were not prepared to make the sacrifices of lesser things, which is the test of the disciple, in order to secure the greater blessing. They undervalued what, to the master of the house, was of immense value.

And so the servants were told to go out quickly and find other guests - the poor, maimed, blind and lame. How different these were from the earlier guests. As the Lord said, "The publicans and the harlots go into the kingdom of God before you" (Matthew 21:31). These would be naturally reluctant to come; they would be out of their element at such an event. And so the servant was instructed to compel them - not by force, but by persuasion. Perhaps this is an illustration of the work of the Holy Spirit in the world today as the convicting force behind the gospel message (John 16:8). Without His work, the word of the gospel would lack its power to save.

Wider and wider the search went, looking for guests who would come and fill the house. They went to the streets and the lanes, then to the highways, even to those sitting in the hedges - "unto the uttermost part of the earth" (Acts 1:8). No one was excluded in this widespread invitation to the great supper. Surely indeed the rejection by Israel has been the blessing of the Gentiles of every tribe and nation.

Judgement

In the accounts in both Matthew and Luke, the rejection of the invitation provoked the anger of the host. This is a reminder to us that the longsuffering and patience of God does not in any way negate His great anger against those who would dare to refuse the Son. His anger is fierce and none can withstand it (Revelation 6:17). The householder's declaration that "none of those men which were bidden shall taste of my supper" was severe and final. So also was the Lord's word about Israel's failure to enter into Canaan in Hebrews 3:11, "I sware in My wrath, they shall not enter into My rest". "It is a fearful thing to fall into the hands of the living God" (Hebrews 10:31).

In Matthew's parable, the king's anger erupted in judgement on two occasions. The first was instant "eye-for-an-eye" destruction by his army of those who had murdered his servants. This may have foretold the destruction of Jerusalem under the Roman commander Titus in the year 70 A.D. as being an early judgement on Israel for their rejection of their Messiah and their persecution of His servants. God will avenge His own.

But there was also a later judgement: It was carried out on a guest who had come to the supper but had not taken to himself the required wedding attire (which would have been provided to him). This was only brought to light when the king himself appeared to welcome the guests. The man was called to account and was "speechless" before the king. He had no excuse. And so he was cast from the brightness of the marriage feast and the presence of the king into outer darkness. So will be the judgement, when the Lord comes, on those who seek access on any basis other than the imputed righteousness of Christ: This is, as Paul described it, "not having a righteousness of mine own" (Philippians 3:9). No one will stand before God in that future day on his own merit, no matter how great that might appear to be. Only the righteousness of Christ which is by faith, by virtue of His completed redemptive work, will be acceptable.

No judgement is referred to in the Luke passage on the other invited guests who did not come. But what is portrayed is the loss of privilege and blessing that they suffered. The kingdom of God is a place of privilege, but only for those who respond in obedience to the words of the Lord. Where there is a lack of response, even if not outright disobedience, the Lord may well determine to carry out His purposes through others, to our great loss ("... that no one take thy crown" Revelation 3:11).

May Israel's loss of blessing, as seen by our understanding of the parable of the king's marriage feast and the Lord's account of the great supper, help us to realize the great blessing that has now been directed toward us, and the serious consequences of our being unresponsive to it as they were.

CHAPTER TWELVE: THE KINGDOM OF HEAVEN

IN MATTHEW CHAPTER 13 the Lord Jesus likened the kingdom of heaven to a man who sowed good seed in his field (verse 24); to a grain of mustard seed (verse 31); to leaven (verse 33); to a treasure hidden in a field (verse 44); to a merchant seeking goodly pearls (verse 45); and to a net cast into the sea (verse 47).

We propose to consider these six parables in relation to truths concerning the kingdom of heaven. Because of space constraints a straightforward exposition of a particular view is offered for consideration, leaving the thoughtful reader to compare alternatives from other sources. The viewpoint suggested is that the Lord's message through these parables referred in each case to the kingdom of heaven as His future millennial reign (Revelation 20:4,6); although the parables throw light on the divine strategy through which in due course the millennial reign will be brought about. That the Lord referred elsewhere to the kingdom of heaven in this sense is illustrated by Matthew 8:11: "I say unto you, that many shall come from the east and the west, and shall Sit down with Abraham, and Isaac, and Jacob, in the kingdom of heaven". From the parallel reference in Luke 13:28,29 it will be noted that the term "kingdom of God" is used instead of "kingdom of heaven". Evidently, then, the future thousand-year reign of Christ is described variously as the kingdom of heaven or the kingdom of God: the rule of the heavens or the rule of God in this world.

The relevance of the six parables under discussion becomes clearer when we recall the general Jewish expectation in the time of the Lord that Messiah would at that time come to establish His kingdom (Luke 19:11). This was reflected when after the feeding of the five thousand the people "were about to come and take Him by force, to make Him king" (John 6:15). Even after the Lord's resurrection the apostles were still asking, "Lord, dost Thou at this time restore the kingdom to Israel?" (Acts 1:6). In the parables of Matthew 13, therefore, the Lord was putting the Messianic hope of the kingdom of heaven in true perspective. It was a realistic hope, as predicted by the prophets, but it would not be brought about in the way many expected. It would be achieved through the process of God's redemptive purposes in Christ. The millennial kingdom of heaven would ultimately be established as one of the great objectives of that process. These parables figuratively illustrate certain aspects of the divine plan which will lead finally to Messiah's reign in this world for one thousand years.

Tares and Wheat (verses 24-30) and Drag-net (verses 47-50)

These two parables are considered together because they convey essentially the same message; in both cases also the Lord explained their meaning. "Explain unto us the parable of the tares of the field", the disciples asked Him. The story was simple and vivid. They could readily visualize the field in which good seed was sown, and relate to the vindictive action of an enemy who secretly sowed tares (or darnel) among the good seed. The disciples would appreciate the point that in early stages of growth it was difficult to distinguish wheat from tares. They could also understand the householder's wisdom in letting both grow until the harvest, lest the good should be destroyed in attempting to uproot the bad. When harvest came, however, the tares were bound in separate bundles to be burned; the wheat was gathered into the barn.

The Lord's interpretation of the parable addressed the perplexing problem of God's permission of continuing evil in the world. Human society world-wide reflects the co-existence of good and evil. Why is evil tolerated by God generation after generation? Why does He not intervene to eradicate it and bring about an order of things where truth, right and goodness prevail? A question re-echoed by many through the centuries, as when the Psalmist cried, "LORD, how long shall the wicked, how long shall the wicked triumph?" (Psalm 94:3). The answer is hidden deep in the counsels of an infinitely wise and loving God. Nevertheless the parable of the tares confirms that relief will certainly come at "the consummation of the age", in God's predetermined time. Faith willingly accepts this revelation of the plan to which God is working, and joyfully "greets from afar" the promised coming of the Son of Man: then, at long last, "shall the Sun of righteousness arise with healing in His wings" (Malachi 4:2).

Meantime God's Word brings spiritual fruitfulness in the lives of "the sons of the kingdom", the "wheat" of the parable. God also allows the continuing activity of the enemy Satan, which produces "sons of the evil one", the "tares" of the parable. In view of the similarity between tares and wheat, "the sons of the evil one" may well include people of religious profession whose character and behaviour bear some resemblance to true disciples of Christ.

Incidentally, it may be helpful to point out that the parable of the tares has often been misapplied to support the idea that the true believer may in our time join in church association with people who are not disciples of Christ. Many scriptures confirm that this is not in accordance with God's revealed plan for corporate Christian worship and witness today; illustrating the importance of interpreting the Lord's parables in harmony with the broad principles of God's Word.

However, coming back to the parable of the drag-net, the Lord's explanation again makes the point that it is in "the consummation of the age" that the wicked will be severed from the righteous. The Greek word translated "consummation" in the marginal reading of Matthew 13:49 (RV) "signifies a bringing to completion together, marking the completion ... of the various parts of a scheme" (W.E. Vine). In the context of this parable we understand the expression points to the coming of the Lord Jesus as Son of Man to take His power and reign. The parable describes how the drag-net was cast into the sea, and gathered of every kind. When drawn up on to the beach the catch was divided into good and bad, representing the righteous and the wicked; in this case a general distinction, rather than the previous emphasis on "sons of evil" with a religious profession. Again the Lord declared the judgement and sad destiny of the wicked: "cast ... into the furnace of fife: there shall be the weeping and gnashing of teeth" (verse 50). Solemn truth from the lips of the Lamb of Calvary!

The Mustard Seed (verses 31,32)

The essential point of this short parable is the contrast between the smallness of the seed and the size of the tree which it produces: "it becometh a tree, so that the birds of the heaven come and lodge in the branches thereof". This instructs those with ears to hear that the kingdom of heaven would not be brought about by great political forces such as Jewish nationalism. It would ultimately develop from what seemed to the worldly-minded of no significance, the despised Prophet of Nazareth, who in meekness and lowliness of heart declared among them the principles of His future kingdom. He personified in their midst the moral glories of that kingdom (Luke 17:21 RV margin). He must Himself, like the mustard seed, fall into the ground and die (compare John 12:24) before the great purpose of the millennial kingdom could be brought about. For the new covenant with the house of Israel which will then obtain (Jeremiah 31:31-34) could never be introduced until He had put away sin by the sacrifice of Himself (Hebrews 9:26).

With that in view He had humbled Himself in obedience; "wherefore also God highly exalted Him ... that in the name of Jesus every knee should bow" (Philippians 2:8-10). His universal authority will be acknowledged when heaven's role is established on earth in that future kingdom; illustrated in the parable by a tree in whose branches birds could lodge; so will His kingdom provide ample for every need of all earth's peoples.

The Leaven (verse 33)

A woman hid leaven in three measures of meal until it was all leavened. The Lord likened this to the kingdom of heaven. In what way, we wonder? Again let us keep to the main point of the illustration, the unseen working of the leaven until it spreads through all three measures of meal. The emphasis is on the inner, unseen work of God in the heart, a vital feature of Christ's future kingdom. It will not merely be a kingdom established by Christ's almighty power, although universal subjection will indeed be imposed. Accompanying this will be a work of the Holy Spirit in people's hearts through the Word of God. This will result in all mankind being pervaded by the knowledge of God.

As to Israel we read: "I will put My law in their inward parts, and in their heart will I write it ... and they shall teach no more ... every man his brother, saying, Know the LORD: for they shall all know Me" (Jeremiah 31:33,34). As to the Gentile nations, "the earth shall be filled with the knowledge of the glory of the LORD, as the waters cover the sea" (Habbakuk 2:14).

The parable of the leaven impresses us with the truth that the rule of the heavens in this world will bring the universal knowledge of God. Man's highest end is to glorify God. Through recognition of this in the "hidden man of the heart", human society worldwide will enjoy the blessed fruits of the fear of the Lord which is the beginning of wisdom. Consequently there will be a depth of allegiance to Messiah's rule, a spiritual assent to its righteous principles, which will give stability to the world order in those times of the restoration of all things (Acts 3:21).

The Treasure and the Pearl (verses 44-46)

These two parables have in common the discovery of something immensely valuable, for which a sacrificial price was paid. To secure the treasure, the man bought the field at the cost of all that he had; at similar cost, the merchant bought the pearl of great price. Do not the man and the merchant both represent the Lord Jesus, who was cut off and had nothing at Calvary so that He could redeem to Himself a people for His own possession? Can we distinguish two particular groups among the multitude of the redeemed which might answer to the treasure and the pearl?

Israel as a redeemed nation is described in millennial times as "a crown of beauty in the hand of the LORD, and a royal diadem in the hand of thy God" (Isaiah 62:3). Again, "the Church, which is His Body, the fulness of Him that filleth all in all" (Ephesians 1:22,23) stands uniquely in glorious relationship to Christ. Both Israel and the Church will feature distinctively in the millennial scene. As the Lord's vision pierced future centuries towards the establishment of the kingdom of heaven in His millennial reign, was He anticipating also the development of these associated divine purposes.

ABOUT THE AUTHORS

Did you love *Heavenly Meanings - The Parables of Jesus*? Then you should read *Different Discipleship: Jesus' Sermon on the Mount*[1] by Hayes Press and Alan Toms!

Different relationships ... Different priorities .... Different perspectives ... Different standards ... Different actions! A practical and challenging 12-module study complete with questions and prayer prompts on the "Sermon on the Mount" for followers and would-be followers of Jesus. What makes Jesus and his followers "different"? Find out why this revolutionary, life-changing sermon is why Jesus Christ is regarded as one of the world's most important teachers, even by those who don't follow him as their Lord and Saviour.

---

1. https://books2read.com/u/31gkYv

2. https://books2read.com/u/31gkYv

Also by Hayes Press

Bible Studies
Bible Studies 1990 - First Samuel
Bible Studies 1991 - The First Letter of Paul to the Corinthians
Bible Studies 1993 - Second Samuel
Bible Studies 1994 - The Establishment and Development of Churches of God
Bible Studies 1995 - The Kings of Judah and Israel from Solomon to Asa
Bible Studies 1992 - The Second Letter of Paul to the Corinthians

Needed Truth
Needed Truth 1888
Needed Truth 2001
Needed Truth 2002
Needed Truth 2003
Needed Truth 2004
Needed Truth 2005
Needed Truth 2006
Needed Truth 2007
Needed Truth 2008
Needed Truth 2009
Needed Truth 2010

Needed Truth 2011
Needed Truth 2012
Needed Truth 1888-1988: A Centenary Review of Major Themes

Old Testament Commentary Series
The Life of King David: From Shepherd Boy to Sovereign:
The Life of Moses: God's Chosen Deliverer

Spiritual Warfare
Spiritual Warfare: Satan and His Kingdom

Training for Service
Different Discipleship: Jesus' Sermon on the Mount

Standalone
The Road Through Calvary: 40 Devotional Readings
Lovers of God's House
The House of God: Past, Present and Future
What is the Kingdom of God?
Knowing God: His Names and Nature
Churches of God: Their Biblical Constitution and Functions
Four Books About Jesus
Collected Writings On ... Exploring Biblical Fellowship
Collected Writings On ... Exploring Biblical Hope
Collected Writings On ... The Cross of Christ
Builders for God

Collected Writings On ... Exploring Biblical Faithfulness
Collected Writings On ... Exploring Biblical Joy
Possessing the Land: Spiritual Lessons from Joshua
Collected Writings On ... Exploring Biblical Holiness
Collected Writings On ... Exploring Biblical Faith
Collected Writings On ... Exploring Biblical Love
These Three Remain...Exploring Biblical Faith, Hope and Love
The Teaching and Testimony of the Apostles
Pressure Points - Biblical Advice for 20 of Life's Biggest Challenges
More Than a Saviour: Exploring the Person and Work of Jesus
Exploring The Psalms: Volumes 1-4
The Faith: Outlines of Scripture Doctrine
Key Doctrines of the Christian Gospel
Is There a Purpose to Life?
An Introduction to Bible Covenants
The Hidden Christ - Volume 2: Types and Shadows in Offerings and Sacrifices
The Hidden Christ Volume 1: Types and Shadows in the Old Testament
The Hidden Christ - Volume 3: Types and Shadows in Genesis
Heavenly Meanings - The Parables of Jesus
Fisherman to Follower: The Life and Teaching of Simon Peter
Called to Serve: Lessons from the Levites
Needed Truth 2017 Issue 1
The Breaking of the Bread: Its History, Its Observance, Its Meaning
Great Spiritual Revivals
An Introduction to the Book of Hebrews
The Holy Spirit and the Believer
Exploring The Psalms: Volume 1 - Thoughts on Key Themes
Exploring The Psalms: Volume 2 - Exploring Key Elements
Exploring the Psalms: Volume 3 - Surveying Key Sections
The Psalms: Volume 4 - Savouring Choice Selections
Profiles of the Prophets

The Hidden Christ - Volumes 1-4 Box Set
The Hidden Christ - Volume 4: Types and Shadows in Israel's Tabernacle
Baptism - Its Meaning and Teaching
Conflict and Controversy in the Church of God in Corinth
In the Shadow of Calvary: A Bible Study of John 12-17
Sparkling Facets: Bible Names and Titles of Jesus
A Little Book About Being Christlike
Keys to Church Growth
Back to Basics: A Study of Core Bible Teaching and Practice
An Introduction to the Holy Spirit
Israel and the Church in Bible Prophecy
"Growth and Fruit" and Other Writings by John Drain
15 Hot Topics For Today's Christian
Needed Truth Volume 2 1889
Studies on the Return of Christ
Studies on the Resurrection of Christ
Needed Truth Volume 3 1890
The Nations of the Old Testament: Their Relationship with Israel and Bible Prophecy
The Message of the Minor Prophets
The Bible - Its Inspiration and Authority
Lessons from Ezra and Nehemiah
A Bible Study of God's Names For His People
Moses in One Hour
Abundant Christianity
Prayer in the New Testament
The Battle: An Anthology of Spiritual Warfare - Volume 1
In the Beginning: Bible Studies in Genesis
Chief of Sinners! The Life of the Apostle Paul
Studies in the Book of Revelation

About the Publisher

Hayes Press (www.hayespress.org) is a registered charity in the United Kingdom, whose primary mission is to disseminate the Word of God, mainly through literature. It is one of the largest distributors of gospel tracts and leaflets in the United Kingdom, with over 100 titles and hundreds of thousands despatched annually. In addition to paperbacks and eBooks, Hayes Press also publishes Plus Eagles Wings, a fun and educational Bible magazine for children, and Golden Bells, a popular daily Bible reading calendar in wall or desk formats. Also available are over 100 Bibles in many different versions, shapes and sizes, Bible text posters and much more!